Margot Fonteyn

Anne Sebba

Illustrated by Valerie Littlewood

Julia MacRae Books
A division of Franklin Watts

Also by Anne Sebba
MOTHER TERESA
(Blackbird Books)

Text © 1983 Anne Sebba
Illustrations © 1983 Valerie Littlewood
All rights reserved
First published in Great Britain 1983 by
Julia MacRae Books
A division of Franklin Watts Ltd
12a Golden Square, London W1R 4BA
and Franklin Watts Inc.
387 Park Avenue South, New York 10016.

British Library Cataloguing in Publication Data
Sebba, Anne
   Margot Fonteyn.—(Blackbird series)
   1. Fonteyn, *Dame* Margot   2. Dancers
   —Biography—Juvenile literature
   792.8'092'4   GV1785.F63
ISBN 0–86203–118–4 UK edition
ISBN 0–531–04603–6 US edition

Phototypeset by Ace Filmsetting Ltd, Frome, Somerset
Made and printed in Great Britain by
Camelot Press, Southampton

Chapter 1

In a Chinese newspaper of 1929 the
following short article appeared:
'Miss Peggy Hookham was easily
the hit of the performance with her
clever dancing, the little girl's
footwork being especially striking in
the dance of a Turkish slave girl
where she jangled her tambourine
and flung herself into the dance with
a gay abandon rare in such a
young dancer.'

Peggy, the little girl in question, was a round-faced, almost podgy nine year-old with short, black hair and a fringe. She was rather silent, with few friends her own age, and was fussy about her food. She was in China because her father's work had taken the family there.

It was during the stay in China that Peggy began to take dancing classes seriously. After school hours she and a friend took lessons from three Russian dancers and Peggy was soon fired by an enthusiasm to be the best pupil in the room. After many years of hard work Peggy Hookham became the legendary Margot Fonteyn, for many people the best dancer in the world.

In fact, ballet lessons had begun even earlier. Peggy was born on May 18th, 1919, in Reigate, Surrey, but the family soon moved to Ealing, just outside London. One day Peggy's father suggested that deportment lessons might be a good idea for his daughter, and so Peggy was taken to the Ealing Dancing

Academy of Miss Grace Bosustow.
She loved the classes from the start.
By the time she was six, Peggy had
won a pink sash for dancing the
best Polka in her class.

Although Peggy learnt much from

her Russian teachers in China, her mother realised that if she were to become a serious ballerina she must train in England. They returned to live in London where the best teacher, Mrs. Hookham decided, would be Princess Seraphine Astafieva.

At first the elderly Princess, also Russian, refused to take her. But Peggy's mother begged: "You must accept my daughter. I have brought her six thousand miles all the way from China to study with you." Astafieva soon recognised her new pupil's talent and taught her, above all, how to make difficult steps look easy.

Next, Peggy's mother decided that her fourteen-year-old daughter should be seen by the school of the Old Vic and Sadler's Wells theatres in North London. "But I'm not nearly ready yet," the young girl protested. However, the ten minute audition took place with Peggy barefoot and wearing just a petticoat. She was accepted at the school.

From now on Miss Ninette de Valois, the Director of the Vic-Wells school, took charge of Peggy's dancing career. This meant that Mrs. Hookham, who had always taken a close interest in her daughter's progress, could no longer

watch her classes. As Peggy and her
mother lived in Kensington Peggy
had to travel across London every
day to and from her new ballet
school.

The students wore plum-coloured
silk tunics with black tights and
were expected to work very hard.

The hour-long morning class included *barre* work and centre practice, and the teachers carried a light cane partly for beating time but sometimes to give a sharp whack to flagging legs or a drooping hand.

For lunch, the students usually ate just a roll and butter with a slice of cheese, and perhaps a packet of nuts and raisins, in a small canteen in the theatre bar. If Miss de Valois was not looking, they would tuck into a chocolate and cream walnut whip.

The afternoons were filled with more lessons as well as rehearsals for some of the students who were lucky enough to have a small part in

the latest performance. Whenever
the dancers were moving around the
theatre it was a firm rule that they
must wear dressing gowns to cover
their short tunics in case visitors
caught a glimpse of their legs.

Margot took her work very
seriously. But she was greatly
teased whenever she was spotted

quietly practising her pirouettes or arabesques in a corner.

Just four weeks after joining the company came a most thrilling moment. A postcard arrived inviting Peggy to make her debut as the third snowflake of the second group on the left in 'The Nutcracker Suite'. According to Mrs. Hookham Peggy was in such a state of excitement on receiving the postcard that their neighbours in the flat below nearly complained about the noise. Although she was very nervous at the first performance, her spirit was stirred. "From this moment on there could be no going back," she said later.

Chapter 2

It was at this time that the young dancer invented her stage name, Margot Fonteyn. Margot was simply a more exotic form of Margaret, the name she was christened, and Fonteyn came from her mother's Brazilian surname, Fontes. "You watch this child, she's going to be a very great dancer," Miss de Valois told a friend. "But she's a perfect little devil—needs a lot of discipline."

Perhaps Miss de Valois was.
thinking of Margot's dislike of *pointe*
work. Unless a strict eye was kept on
her she would wear old, soft shoes in
place of uncomfortable but firm
new ones, necessary for dancing
en pointes.

Putting on stage make-up was
another trick for Margot to learn.
Some of the older girls in the
company took Margot off one day
and showed her where to buy special
sticks of face cream. They also
taught her how to make false
eyelashes by melting black wax in a
spoon over a candle and applying it
carefully with a hairpin to a natural

lash. This led to big blobs which sometimes fell into a dancer's eye during a ballet. It seems that Margot was not very good at making-up at first as someone in the audience was once heard to shout: "Fifteen—that girl looks more like fifty."

A year after joining the school
Margot became a member of the
company and no longer a student.
She was hailed by one critic as the
'Dazzling New Star of the Future'.
At this time Frederick Ashton

joined the Vic-Wells. As the choreographer he created the steps and movements for the ballets and Margot was fortunate to work with him, as well as performing with such outstanding partners as the Australian, Robert Helpmann. Although frightened of Robert Helpmann at first, Margot danced with him successfully for fourteen years.

Gradually, Margot was being given more and more solo roles. On January 19th, 1937, she danced Giselle, one of the most demanding roles of the great classical ballets. Giselle, a young peasant girl, has two sweethearts, Hilarion, a game-

keeper and Albrecht, a handsome young duke whom she believed also to be a peasant because of his disguise. When she discovers that Albrecht is a duke, already betrothed to a princess, she is overcome by grief and dashes about the stage in a dance of utter madness. Finally she snatches Albrecht's sword to kill herself. It was a role Margot dreaded, fearing she would not be good enough. But she was magnificent, and continued to dance the part for many years. Her hard work rehearsing the famous 'mad' scene paid off as her acting was considered as fine as any of the great stage actresses of the day.

Chapter 3

In 1939 war was declared and the Sadler's Wells Ballet, as it was now known, was immediately disbanded. The government had decided to close all places of entertainment. Two weeks later, however, the Company was recalled for a tour and everyone complained of very sore muscles and bruised toes after fourteen days of not using them.

During the next five years of war

Margot and her fellow dancers often performed at military camps. Many a hearty soldier complained about having to watch fancy ballet dancing. But others, who had never been able to see ballet before, were thrilled at the new opportunity. Previously ballets were seen only by a privileged few, mostly in London. Now there were tours in all parts of Britain with just two pianos instead of the usual full orchestra as an accompaniment.

In May 1940, the Sadler's Wells ballet set off on a tour of Holland, Belgium and France. Although the war was raging on, it was hoped that the travelling entertainers would help stiffen the people's courage in the fight against Germany.

The first performance was greeted with tremendous enthusiasm and the cast was showered with tulips. But, after four days dancing, the German army invaded and the Company wondered how they would get back to England.

The following night two buses drew up outside the hotel; everyone clambered aboard without a clue as to where they were going. Somehow, after four days of worried waiting and terrifying travelling, they arrived at a harbour. Feeling cold and scared, the bedraggled group was bundled into the hold of a cargo

boat and, twenty-four hours later,
after rough seas and high waves, all
arrived safely back in England.

They later discovered they had left
behind the scenery, costumes and
music for six ballets.

Back in England Margot danced harder than ever, giving nine or ten performances a week—a routine unheard of for today's ballet dancers. Food was strictly rationed and so she was most grateful to her fans who sent her little parcels of sugar, chocolate and butter, which dancers badly needed to keep up their energy. In spite of the fear of bombs falling the theatre was full every night throughout the war.

The Sadler's Wells Ballet was rewarded for its hard wartime work when it was invited to make its home at the Royal Opera House in Covent Garden. The first performance there was to be a grand new production of

'Sleeping Beauty', with Margot in the title role.

23

"There were so many 'royals' present at the opening that when I came to the last presentation curtsy I was dizzy from bobbing up and down," Margot said later. "I almost overbalanced when, to my astonishment Princess Margaret, then aged fifteen, expertly and unobtrusively steadied me with her handshake." The ballet was a triumph, the first of many huge successes for the Company in its new home.

But then, in the middle of a performance, she slipped and hurt her ankle. Her leg was put in plaster and she was ordered not to dance again for at least three months. Margot was heartbroken; now she would not be able to dance Cinderella, a new role which she had worked on for six months. She went away to Paris to rest, unable to watch someone else in the part.

In 1949 the Company danced for the first time in America. The performances ended with loud roars of applause and curtain call after curtain call. In Washington, however, several of the dancers, including Margot, fell flat on their faces on the slippery stage. But the Company nonetheless won fame and glory in the U.S.A.

Chapter 4

Just as Margot Fonteyn was being hailed as an international star two disasters struck. In the winter of 1951, she was absent for several months with a strained foot. The following year she fell ill with diptheria. This time she was away from the stage for five months. When she finally returned the welcome was overwhelming, with flowers spread thickly across the sixty-foot width of the stage. The crowds were determined to show Margot that they loved her.

So, too, was one particular fan, a man with dark eyes of whom Margot had often dreamed. He also used flowers to declare his love for her— delivering one hundred red roses to her tiny dressing room. Dr. Roberto (Tito) Arias, a diplomat from

Panama, had first met Margot when he studied at Cambridge before the war. They had not seen each other for many years, but now he followed her round the world wherever she was dancing. So the romance grew.

The couple were married in Paris on February 6, 1955. The night before, Margot had danced one of her favourite roles, the shepherdess, Chloë in 'Daphnis and Chloë'. Daphnis, a young shepherd, was very deeply in love with Chloë. But while they were out one day she was seized by a group of pirates. Daphnis, in terrible torment at the loss of his loved one, prayed at the

altar of the God Pan for help. When
he awoke out of his trance, Chloë
was returned to him. The happy
pair then made their solemn
marriage vows before Pan's altar,
and all the villagers performed a
gay dance to celebrate. On this

occasion when the villagers entered, their scarves were full of confetti and rose petals to throw at Margot, the new bride both on stage and in real life. The audience quickly joined in, throwing their own streamers. Margot turned to them and said: "If I am one tenth as happy in my future life as I am tonight I shall be a very lucky girl. I thank you from the bottom of my heart for all your kind wishes."

Marriage did not keep Margot from her beloved ballet. Just before her wedding she was told she was to be the new President of the Royal Academy of Dancing. Although reluctant to accept at first she has

worked hard and successfully at the
job ever since.

Soon after the appointment
Margot was made a Dame
Commander of the British Empire—

the first dancer to win that award in
mid-career. The stage hands at
New York's Metropolitan Opera

House, who had nicknamed her 'Dimples' because of her warm smile, now called her 'Dame Dimples'.

She had another job, too, Ambassadress, as her husband Tito was appointed Panamanian Ambassador to London in 1956. She found one of the most difficult aspects of this job was remembering all the names of the many other diplomats and their wives whom she had to meet.

In between these duties Margot Fonteyn the ballerina was giving pleasure to millions all over the world. In 1957 the Company became The Royal Ballet and, during tours

of Australia and Brazil, its leading
lady was certainly treated like
royalty. Then, in the spring of 1959,
the Company toured New Zealand

and Japan. Finding long separations
from her husband unbearable,
Margot was very excited when the
day came for her to join him in
Panama.

But the adventures of the next ten
days were more like a spy thriller
than a holiday. Tito was plotting a
revolution for his country. But when
this went wrong he managed to
escape by boat, leaving Margot
cruising round some islands in
another boat acting as a decoy. A
day later she was arrested and
taken to gaol. Her room in prison
was not an ordinary cell. It
contained roses from the prison
garden and she was offered a radio,

SEARCH GOES

BALLERINA IS
HELD HOSTAGE

Sea hunt for husb

FON
RE

DRAMA

in case she wanted music for dancing! But, after a day, with no explanation, she was suddenly led out of a side entrance of the prison, driven to the airport and put on the first plane out of the country. It was several months before she was able to meet up with Tito again.

Chapter 5

During the 1950's, the pain in her left foot grew so bad that she was forced to give up dancing one or two of her most difficult roles. She was almost in despair about her foot when, just before one of the Company's most important tours to Russia, a new treatment cured it.

Dancing in Russia, a country so full of balletic traditions, was a very moving experience for Margot and her fellow dancers. While there she heard that a Russian male dancer had left the great Kirov Company and asked for permission to live in the West. He was Rudolf Nureyev, then aged just twenty-three.

Nureyev was soon invited to London. He was determined to dance with Margot Fonteyn, the world's number one ballerina, even though he was twenty years younger than she. At first, Margot did not like the idea at all. "But I discussed it with Tito and we came to the conclusion that Rudolf was going to be the big sensation of the next year and I had better get on the bandwagon or else get out," said Margot. Also, dancing solo never much appealed to her. "I really like depending on my partner for inspiration and passion," she says. She found plenty of both these with the young Russian.

Soon the great pair began rehearsing together. Margot, the established ballerina was very modest and allowed the young boy to teach her one or two things. Nureyev worked very hard and even Margot was amazed at his energy.

In February 1962 the two
appeared on stage together for the
first time in 'Giselle'. They made
such an unforgettable partnership
that ballet fans begged to see them
again and again. At the end of the
first performance, as the crowd
cheered wildly and stamped their

feet, Nureyev dropped to one knee and kissed Margot's hand. The gesture seemed to say: 'Thank you for your partnership, it was marvellous dancing with you.' At the end of the London season that year, Margot took twenty-six curtain calls.

In spite of their age difference Fonteyn and Nureyev went on to create a fabulous partnership, dancing most of the famous classical ballets as well as some new ones written specially for them. But in the summer of 1964 tragedy struck.

Margot was dancing in the city of Bath when news reached her late at night that her husband had been shot in Panama. Bravely, she went on stage the following day to dance a matinée and an evening performance and even gave an encore when the audience demanded it. But she rushed away afterwards to fly to her husband's bedside.

Many anxious weeks passed before he seemed to be out of danger and well enough to travel to Stoke Mandeville hospital in England for further treatment. He would never be able to walk again, but he might be able to use his arms and hands a little and he had to be taught how to speak again.

Margot sat up with her husband night after night even though

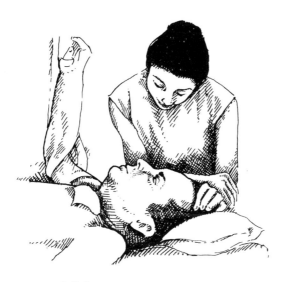

doctors told her to get some rest. "They underestimated the advantage, in times of stress, of a long ballet discipline," she explained.

In time, Tito returned to Panama and Margot was as much in demand as ever. In 1967 Roland Petit, a French choreographer, created a ballet especially for her and Nureyev. Her entrance for this was

from a trap-door in the middle of a ramp at the back of the set. To reach it she had to crawl on her hands and knees through a sort of tunnel for about thirty feet. Quite a feat for a ballet dancer celebrating her forty-eighth birthday on the opening night! No wonder the New York audience sang 'Happy Birthday' at the end of the evening.

When Margot found she could no longer buy pure silk tights and would have to wear the hated nylon ones, she nearly gave up dancing. But another famous ballerina, Svetlana Beriosova, came to her rescue and passed on her own silk tights to Fonteyn.

On May 23rd, 1979, to celebrate her 60th birthday, Sir Frederick Ashton wrote a special ballet for her. It was called 'Salut D'amour' (A Tribute of Love) and was made up of different passages from her favourite ballets. This was the last time she danced at Covent Garden, but she seemed unable to give up ballet completely. Even after this 'farewell performance' she accepted an invitation from Nureyev to dance the role of Lady Capulet in Romeo and Juliet with him.

Today, she also has a new career, that of farmer in Panama. She is as happy as ever looking after her cattle herd, her ranch and, of course, her husband.